KEEPING YOUR DAY JOB AND YOUR DAY Dream

KENNETH BRYANT II

KEEPING YOUR DAY JOB AND YOUR DAY *Dream*

KENNETH BRYANT II

Publisher:
MEWE, LLC
www.mewellc.com

First Edition
ISBN: 9781733438308

Library of Congress Control Number: 2019912139

Printed in the United States of America.

To my dear sister, the late Rebecca White, my dear brother, the late Shelby Henson, and my dear niece, the late Cadence Able. Your lives inspired me forward, until we meet again.

Acknowledgments

I would like to thank my dear wife, Ebony Michelle for loving me, believing in me, and supporting me. And our children; Kenneth III and Diana, for making me the luckiest father in the world!

I also want to acknowledge all my family: Kenneth and Cecile (Mom & Dad), Vicki (mom in-love), Jonathan and Kristy (siblings), Tiffany, Fatima, Greg, and Sylvester (siblings-in-love), all my nieces and nephews, Gary and Trudie Bolles / Hezekiah and Jeanette Pressley (Godparents) and all of my (many) God-brothers and sisters.

Lastly, I want to thank some very special friends who are like brothers: Jon-Jon, Mike, Isaac, and Raymond.

Thank you all for believing in me throughout the years!

Foreword

You can't!

You can't read this book and not reflect on your own journey till now. The hope of this book is that your reflection will grow and reignite that dream you've carried all your life. The dream that got sidetracked because of "either-or" thinking but will resurrect with "both-and" thinking.

My friend Kenneth Bryant II wrote *Keeping Your Day Job and Your Day Dream* not as an abstract thought, rather this personifies who he is. I've known Kenneth for almost two decades and what I like about him is that he made a choice not to be limited. In this book, his pragmatism, in part parable and part encouragement, will nudge you with your *why* for being placed on this planet.

This book made me reflect on my life. I have worked at a daycare, Goodwill, breakfast cook, dishwasher, janitor, school monitor, youth pastor, senior pastor, mental health clinician, college president and now as a leadership consultant – can you see the zig-zag?

Looking back, I can connect the dots. But moving forward from one station in life to another – not so much.

This book will connect the dots. Resurrect your dreams. Enlarge your desires. Awaken the dormant and make you *dream out loud.*

You can!

Sam Chand
Leadership Consultant and Author
www.samchand.com

Preface

As the oldest child of three siblings, I remember taking long rides in a sedan-styled automobile. As you could imagine, there were many things that three siblings argued about, but one argument that always started, before the trip ever began, was "who is sitting in the middle?" No one wanted to sit in the middle; it was the most uncomfortable part of the ride. On either of the end seats, you had control of the windows, the door locks, and in some cases the air vents. It was akin to sitting in the middle on an airline flight.

In the window seats, you have the obvious concession in the title. And in the aisle seats you have, again the title-concessions. But in the middle seat of the airline flight, there aren't many, if any concessions there. The middle is the proverbial "no-man's land." It is the between, the potential, but not yet. And it is the place where life can be the most challenging. When you are not where you were, but you are not where you envisioned you would be. It is the place where situational, perhaps stress-induced, amnesia can occur. And while you are working to fulfill a dream, you start to forget the dream, and the reason for your toil and labor. Therefore, life, work, the process of realizing a dream, and all things related can start to feel like a personal grind. And now, in the middle, we are tested to push forward in the direction we initially engaged, or to settle in the middle; letting go of hopes to be exceptional and fulfill our dreams.

Some people seize their opportunities and fulfill their dreams early in life. Other people must wait, prepare, work, develop, and persevere so when the opportunity comes, they are ready to seize it! This book is written to inspire all types of people in that liminal space; between pursuing their dream and having it materialize. It's the story of a person that lost touch with all his passions in the liminal space, until he met someone who had made it out of the middle, to the other side.

So, whether you're a retail manager with a passion for photography, a casting director with an enthusiasm for cooking, a session musician with a dream of teaching music education, or anyone working in one field, but dreaming in another, I sincerely hope to give you a coherent and logical reason why you should keep your dream while, at the same time, staying motivated and excelling at your day job. In the end, all our education, work-experience, and the development of skills and your passion come together to do more than we could ever imagine. There is a piece in ancient Hebrew Wisdom Literature that captures this idea: In the morning of your life, sow many seeds, and in the evening of your life, don't slow down; because you don't know which seeds will produce the greatest harvest; the morning seeds, or the evening seeds. It is also possible that both the morning seeds, and evening seeds, will produce an even greater harvest (See Ecclesiastes 11:6).

So, Keep your Day Job, and Your Day Dream...

Kenneth Bryant II

1

WTF or Why?

"Happy Monday," someone lifelessly and sarcastically said as Lance and several other employees from the parking deck staggered into the elevators. Lance thought about how every time people made that joke, he had to resist the urge of causing them physical harm. First, it's so old and played out, and it's like the happy hump day joke. At least, no one laughed; that's always annoying. The polite, "You say something stupid, so now I have to laugh out of pity – that laugh,"

"Someone press floor sixteen!" He shouted from the back of the elevator. Then all of a sudden everyone began yelling at the unfortunate person stuck next to the elevator control panel on a Monday morning.

A surly older gentleman yelled, "Floor eleven, please!"

Some intern from the sales department shouted, "Hey! Three really quick!" The elevator was on the first floor, and he was scared they would pass it, which would make him late for work.

"Floor eight!" shouted a lady with shades, slumped over, leaning on the back wall, clearly hungover from celebrating Sunday's game. "Floor eight!" she shouted again, thinking she had not been heard.

"Press number twenty-one, my man" interjected a food delivery driver.

At this point, even Lance felt sorry for the person next to the elevator panel.

"Floor ayeeeeeeeeetttt!" There it was again, sounding more and more like a threat than a request.

"He's got it; somebody pressed it," Lance replied. At which point he took in the silence that fills the elevator when no one wants to speak or be spoken to.

It's that Monday moment of depression when you are returning to a job you tolerate, but don't enjoy. Sometimes the job is okay but the people are infuriating. Other days, there is such a confluence of negativity, you can't tell if you hate the job because of the people or the people because of your job!

The elevator closed and started moving. Lance was thinking: *I wish I was like Marty, retiring later this week.* He continued reasoning with himself. *It must be nice to get the* f—

"FLOOR EIGHT!" she yelled again as the elevator was approaching the third floor.

At this point, everyone in the elevator responded

simultaneously, "IT'S PRESSED; he's got it, lady! Stop yelling for God's sakes. What is wrong with you?"

I can't even think on the elevator in peace before I get to the dungeon. Maybe I need to go to counseling or something; I really hate feeling like this. Why do I feel like this? Lance thought to himself.

He finally arrived at work and walked by Mildred's desk. She is your typical receptionist employed for her customer service competencies: always positive and sunny. But sometimes Lance found her annoying!

"Happy Monday, Lance. Did that young lady ever get to floor eight?!" Mildred greeted him.

At which point, Lance realized two things: the lady actually didn't get off at floor eight, and his elevator ride didn't magically make him like the "Happy Monday" joke.

"She was on there when I arrived an hour-and-a-half ago," Mildred continued.

Reluctantly, Lance replied, "Good Morning, Mildred, and yes, I think she is still on the elevator, screaming for floor eight. Anything new?"

"Yes, Jennifer wants to see you. I think she wants

you to interview – Kevin Seinfeld!" Mildred said with a most excited expression.

Lance, realizing this interview may cause him to travel somewhere to a warmer climate, responded, "Mildred, are you sure? What would make you think she is giving that story to me?"

"I overheard her talking with some of the board members. She said you were ready, and this opportunity should go to someone who earned it."

That's another reason why Mildred was useful. She was always willing to share the inner-workings of the office if she could trust you.

Lance had learned not to become too excited about matters like this, so he held his joy until he got the official word. Mildred was right. While meeting with Jennifer (Lance's manager and chief editor), it was confirmed he would be interviewing Kevin Seinfeld for www.businessparody.com!

"Fortunately for us Lance, you won't have to travel. Mr. Seinfeld just opened an office here in the downtown area," Jennifer announced. "Not only do we get to send our best journalist to interview Mr. Seinfeld, but we also don't have to pay for airfare and a hotel!"

A very disingenuous "Yayyyyyy" came out of Lance's mouth as he gathered his things. "Thanks, boss," Lance said sincerely as he left the office.

An opportunity to interview the great Kevin Seinfeld – this is awesome. If I do a good job, it might open up new opportunities for promotion at the company. After all, things had really gotten better since Jennifer became the new editor. I hope Mr. Seinfeld is not a jerk or something. Most of the CEO's I talk to could really use a reality check. Hopefully, he is one of the grounded ones.

Lance contacted Mr. Seinfeld's personal assistant and set up a time for the interview. "Thursday at 9 a.m. – understood – and thank you, Ashley. I will see you there."

"Mildred, you're the best. Thanks for the heads up," whispered Lance as Mildred smiled while finishing a client's phone call.

The next few days, Lance spent his time doing further research on Kevin Seinfeld. Everyone knew he was the latest overnight-success businessman. However, Lance, like any good journalist, wanted to ensure the pieces of his past were arranged in such a way that his article would be unique from all the other interviews he had done.

It's really hard to find things about this guy in the

main news sources. It's like he appeared out of thin air a few years ago, Lance thought while researching.

Research on Kevin Seinfeld showed he was virtually a normal, everyday type-of-guy until about six or seven years earlier. Lance began to see many different records on Kevin Seinfeld –kindergarten teacher, electricians union membership, Uber driver. "That can't be right!" Lance said. All of the information seemed to be about different Kevin Seinfeld's from all over the country, not the globally-renowned restaurant CEO and Founder.

I had better sift through this information and sort it out before our interview Thursday. Would hate to reference the wrong history of an interviewee, Lance thought to himself.

When Thursday arrived, Lance was still very confused about the various threads he had put together. "This doesn't make any sense, but I'll get through it. I'll just have to ask him more questions to put my research pieces together." Lance knew how to talk to successful businessmen: simply ask them questions about themselves, and they'll tell you everything they want you to know. As for the other history of their lives (things they don't want you to know), he knew where to go for that type of information.

"Good Morning, I'm Lance from business-parody.com here for Mr. Seinfeld," he announced as he observed the young, vibrant-looking receptionist.

"Good Morning, sir, how are you?" She looked at him smiling. Lance froze without responding as he wasn't used to people waiting for an answer when they asked the question, "How are you?" He stared at Ashley, the receptionist, waiting for instructions. At this point, she repeated her question, "Good Morning, Lance, how are *you* today?"

Lance replied while stuttering as he was thinking of a response. "Uh, uh, fi-fine, I'm good, thanks. Did you need anything from me?"

"Yes, may I have your ID and business card, please? We have some refreshments; please feel free to have some while you wait," Ashley instructed as Lance provided the information.

Lance took a moment to observe the office, the pictures, that music. *Everything is so smooth, relaxing, almost like a spa! And not those spas I uncovered in my investigative piece a few years back – a real relaxing spa.*

"Lance, here is your identification, thank you. Mr.

Seinfeld will be with you in a few minutes," said Ashley.

"Thanks!" Lance replied.

A few minutes went by and soon, Lance heard what he had been waiting for: "He's ready to see you," Ashley announced.

Lance gathered his laptop, notebook, and other interview accouterments and walked into Kevin Seinfeld's office.

To Lance's surprise, the greeting was very gregarious: "Good Morning, Lance, thank you for your patience. We have all types of checks we perform to verify identify and blah, blah, blah. Please have a seat anywhere you would like. We can sit at the conference table, but if you are comfortable being less formal, we can use the sitting area where the couch is located."

Lance opted to conduct the interview in the sitting area thinking, as a journalist would, that Kevin would open up more if he was casual and relaxed. "Here is fine, if that's okay," Lance said as he pointed to the sitting area.

The two began talking, starting with the basic greeting questions, then moving into how long Kevin had been in the restaurant business. Eventually, Lance realized that all of the "other" Kevin Seinfeld(s) he had researched were really the same person. Kevin talked about his time as a school teacher, his passion for the hospitality industry, his stint as a guitarist in a moderately successful jazz fusion band, some of the connections he made as an Uber driver, and many other roles he had throughout his life.

Lance was completely amazed at how varied Kevin's experiences were. Most CEO's work their way up the corporate ladder progressing in a straight line, but this was quite different. Kevin's path was a zigzag, unique, and riddled with all types of segmented career stops and jumps. However, Kevin admittedly kept his dream and passion for the hospitality and service industry alive. His journey to building this multi-million dollar company and becoming the majority-owner sounded like something out of a movie.

The interview concluded, but Lance had a personal question he wanted to ask Kevin. To Lance's disbelief, the story of Kevin's path was less about corporate maneuvering and forming winning political alliances and more about an inspiration to keep working on a long-held dream. *Was it luck? It had to be! Things don't normally happen like that for people,* Lance thought.

As he gathered his things, a couple of dates in his mental timeline overlapped, and he clearly understood something. While Kevin Seinfeld's current organization was a little more than ten years old, it was a combination of a business he started. His original company was bought by his current company but kept him as the CEO. This allowed him to remain the founder since he was still the majority shareholder. Lance continued to think and while computing the years, he astonishingly asked, "You started the original company about thirty-five years ago!?"

"Yes! You are the first reporter to recognize that. Many of them believe I came on the scene in the later acquisition, but I actually started my business a little more than thirty- five years ago," Kevin replied.

"So you have been holding on to a dream to work in the hospitality industry since you were…about… eighteen years old?" said Lance.

"Yep, that's right. Seems like a long time ago, but it went by fast. I suppose everyone says that though." Kevin laughed at his own joke and waited for Lance's follow-up question. He knew it was coming.

"Why did you wait that long for success in this industry? How did you wait that long?" Lance asked in amazement.

"Simple, it was my dream to do it. I always wanted

to have my own company in the hospitality sector. So, I tried many times and failed many times, all while continuing to work in other careers. But I also continued to work my dream as well."

"Work your dream?" Lance responded.

"That's right! Work my dream. One day when I had become a corporate zombie, I asked myself WTF?"

Lance nodded in agreement, "I know right – like what the f—"

"No, no, no, not that! We don't use that kind of language here," Kevin laughed. "I know, I know, investigative reporters aren't afraid to go blue when they have to! WTF – as in what's this for or why am I doing this? Where is it leading? How does this end for me? I didn't want to spend purposeless days working for a paycheck. I had the notion that I can be passionate about what I am doing now or be passionate about what I was learning in an industry, so I could use it to work on my dream."

"WTF, huh?" Lance laughed. "That's a little different from the way I use that expression, but I think the meaning is the same." They both laughed.

"Yeah, it probably is," Kevin acquiesced. Then he

continued, “Lance, not understanding ‘What's This For’ makes work and perhaps life excruciating. An ancient Hebrew proverb intimates the idea that where a vision is not present, people deteriorate (See Proverbs 29:18). I kept saying to myself: this is what I envision, and this is what I am going to work towards. So regardless of what I did for a day job, I still kept my day dream!”

Lance mused over those words and was inspired. But for him, analysis was the order of the day. Any depth of thought spawns a question. “So you worked your job and your dream?”

“That’s exactly right. I used vision and work to keep my dream alive. Besides, it wouldn’t die anyway,” Kevin quipped.

Why, is one of the most important things we never ask. It's one of those questions that, even if you ask it once, and answer it, you will find the need to remind yourself years afterward: what the answer to this question was again. WHY? Simon Sinek gave a Ted Talk several years ago, that became a book, it said great leaders start with why. His premise was that before any business venture, when forming the mission statement, the statement and purpose of business should answer the questions of why before asking anything else (i.e. what, how, when or where).

If I could grab your attention for one moment, whether you continue to read or not, it would be my hope that you ask yourself the question, WHY, in all its transpositions.

Why am I not happy, why am I working, why am I good at this, why am I bad at this, why can't I be great at both, why can't it happen for me, Why, why and more whys?

In addition to asking these questions, I also hope that you get to a truthful answer. Meaning, or purpose, is one of the four fundamental questions of reality. So, as a different exercise, get a journal and write about your dream, write what you see. Did you have one, and forgot it? Turn off the television, deactivate social media, turn off the radio and get to a quiet place where you can "think your own thoughts" (Andrew Cohen, Huffington Post article 2012). Envision where you WANT to be in 10 years and pay special attention to what you want to be DOING in that time.

2

It Wouldn't Die

"It wouldn't die. What do you mean?" Lance asked as Kevin shared his sentiment.

Kevin laughed, "I'm not morbid, but I think of unpursued dreams and ideas as dead. I went through a period where I tried to settle and let it die, but it wouldn't. I call it the 'Horror Movie Syndrome.' When you only dream your dream but don't work your dream, it becomes a nightmare! It becomes the monster that won't die at the end of a horror movie. I am not a fan of the horror film genre, but I have seen a few pieces of classic horror films. One character wore a hockey mask and the characters in that movie did everything they could to kill him, but he just would not die!"

Kevin laughed, "I mean they burned, shot and impaled him. They ran him over and probably some other things I am forgetting. But he would turn up somewhere else, at another time or location. At one point, they thought they got him in the forest, but he reappeared at the cabin. They thought they beat him at an abandoned gas station, but he reappeared somewhere else."

Kevin explained while he continued to laugh: "Horror movies are really disturbing, especially when you are a young child. I could not get that out of my head for the rest of the year!

"In many ways, my dream was like that. It simply would not leave me alone. I tried to forget it, to ignore it. I tried to bury it by accepting the idea that maybe it would not happen for me. I tried to find rest in complacency, putting my dreams in a nursing hospice of life and letting them pass. But they simply would not die. The more I ignored my dream, the more it became the ironic, tormenting memory of something I had yet to experience. Can you imagine living life handcuffed to a zombie? That's the best way to describe living while trying to bury a dream or vision for your life. It never goes away; it's always with you, and it has a tendency to make your life miserable. I concluded that we must dream, but we must also work. However, for dreaming or work to be meaningful, they must be combined. Working alone can become meaningless without a dream, a vision or purpose for your life. Dreaming alone is meaningless and vexing without work. In conclusion, we have to learn to work our dreams! Does that make sense?" Kevin asked.

Lance nodded as he continued to think about his own dreams he had tried to bury or put away. In some cases, he was just trying to work until he had time to resume his attempts to make things happen. But it had been years, and the dangling promise of working on his dream was starting to make his days miserable. He completely identified with that dejected feeling of dragging himself into work and simply going through the motions.

"I understand what you are saying, but sometimes, it just seems easier to give up and just do enough to get by. You know, maybe set the targets a little lower; don't aim for the stars, and be more realistic about the time you have left," Lance responded after contemplating Kevin's words.

"'Give up,' you said! If I have heard that phrase once, I've heard it a million times."

Kevin laughed as he recalled various situations in which giving up seemed like the best option. "I think every person who has ever achieved any level of success has had to deal with the overwhelming temptation to simply give up. It is a real challenge. I have been in that place more than once. But can I share something I learned about the expression 'give up'? It is actually short-hand or texting language for 'Give it up!' As we have done with many expressions, we shorten it because we presume people know the meaning.

"As fans, if we were watching a basketball game where one team is dominating the other by thirty points with only thirty seconds left on the clock, we might say they should just give up. If we are watching a football game and one team is up by twenty-one points with less than a minute left on the clock, we might also say they should just give up. Baseball, as a sport, is a little different; it's not run by a shot clock or a game clock. Nothing keeps time in baseball. I remember my son's little league team was down by nine runs in a state tournament; they had two outs in their final at bat. In baseball, you can keep swinging until someone gets an out. That team rallied to put up ten runs and win the game. They completed what we refer to as a two-out rally!" Kevin spoke with much excitement as he pointed to the picture of him and his son holding the winning trophy.

"Simply put, when we say 'give up' instead of 'giving it up,' we don't always know exactly what we are giving up. For those kids, they would have given up one of the most exciting come-from-behind wins in their young baseball lives. Ironically, the most important word in the phrase is the one we have omitted, the 'it.' Imagine some person encouraging you to give up without knowing what we are actually giving up.

"Would you give it up if the 'it' was a 2.5 million dollar patent idea? Would you give it up if the 'it' was a Grammy, Emmy or Oscar award-winning song, script, or book idea? Would you give it up, if 'it' was research leading to the cure of a terminal illness like cancer or HIV?"

Kevin waited for Lance to really think about his words. Then he continued, "Perhaps we should never give up because we never know what the 'it' is we are forfeiting. And in that sense, 'it' was too expensive for me to give up!"

Lance sighed and responded, "I've never thought about my dream that way. The dream is the 'it' of my life. And if I give that up, I may live with the regret of knowing I really never knew exactly what I was giving up."

Summoning all the humility he could muster – and maybe a little more – knowing he would need it, Lance said, "Kevin, I need to be around more people like you, people who inspire me to work toward my dreams, not bury them. I'd love to continue this conversation for two reasons: I think this is the type of stuff that our readers will want to know about you and your journey. But also, I need this type of dialogue to counteract all the years of self-doubting I have succumbed to."

Kevin replied in a most reassuring tone, "I'd be happy to meet again and continue the conversation.

Schedule our next meeting with Ashley on your way out. I'll make myself available."

"Thank you! Thank you! Thank you so much! I'll make sure to do that. I can't wait to hear the next step in your journey," Lance said in a most exuberant tone.

"Yes, I can't wait to tell about my Double Major Instinct theory," Kevin replied as he returned to his desk to prepare for the next meeting.

"Wait! What?" Lance replied.

"Mr. Seinfeld, your 10:30 is here," Ashley, Kevin's assistant announced over the phone.

"Okay, send them in. See you next week, Lance!" said Kevin.

Lance left the office inspired by what he heard. Even though he was a little confused about what was to come. "Double-Major," he said as he laughed out loud. Lance was grateful he had encountered someone like Kevin who encouraged him in both his job and his dream.

Actions & Endnotes

Did you find it? Did it pop back up after you took some time to think and to imagine? You'll find that it is tied to something you have known all along, or something you have been doing all along. Now, it's time to put a plan together and execute. Your plan won't be perfect, and it's okay. START it! Don't wait another day, another minute, another hour. START it. Yes, you will make mistakes, it may not come together perfectly, it may make a mess of your life.

So, do you need to earn a degree to get there? Do you need a certification to achieve that level of success? Do you need to intern at an origination to get your "proverbial foot in the door?" Identify your actions and start executing your plan.

- Obstacle: I don't know

anyone in the industry: Search for contacts on LinkedIn

- Obstacle: I don't have money to start school or certification: Check out the website Lynda.com and LinkedIn Learning. You can learn information about nearly every professional field for a lot less than attending a university.

- Obstacle: I'm too old to learn something different: You are able to learn! Cell phones may not have existed when you were born, but now you know how to use one. You are not too old to learn!

- Obstacle: Whatever your challenge, there is an answer, a solution! YOU are not the only person that has had this issue. Connect, research, and get inspiration for YOUR game plan and execute!

3

Double-Major Instinct

Lance couldn't wait to find out more about Kevin's philosophy: working your job and your dream. It was a long commute, but once he was out of the car, he dropped his keys into the bag and bolted into the building. "Floor number eight, please," he said to the other person standing in the elevator.

Immediately, he went to the appropriate office suite and saw Ashley, Kevin's executive assistant. He immediately proceeded to her desk. Ashley spoke with a raised voice, "Excuse me, you need to have a seat before going to the office. I will call you when Mr. Seinfeld is ready."

Lance responded as if aggravated, "Look, I have a 9:00 a.m. appointment, and it's already 8:55 a.m. You might as well let me in!"

Ashley replied calmly and professionally, "I understand your point, and I promise we will get to you as soon as possible. But I need to make sure my manager is prepared to see you. Think about it; I'm not doing my job if I simply let people walk to his office, right?"

Lance thought about it for a moment and eventually acceded to Ashley's request. Ashley continued. "Besides, we have coffee, pastries, and other refreshments you can enjoy before your meeting." Lance immediately relaxed at that notion and decided to do as Ashley suggested.

Not long after, Ashley called Lance's name and said, "He's ready to see you now; thanks for your patience." While Lance and Ashley had their share of flirty squabbles, even he had to admit, her courtesy and professionalism were very disarming. "Thanks!" He said as he proceeded into Kevin's office.

"Good Morning, Lance, how are you?

Lance answered right away, "I'm fine – so the Double Major Instinct?"

Kevin let out a patient sigh and responded with humour, "I'm doing well also; thank you for asking." To Lance's irritation, Kevin patiently waited for a response.

Lance said sincerely, "I am so sorry. I was really anxious to continue our conversation and forgot my manners. How are you doing?"

"Lance, I already told you; I'm fine!" They both laughed at the out-of-sequence response.

"So, what were you saying when you walked in?" Kevin asked.

"The Double Major Instinct, what is it? It sounds like the Drum Major Instinct." Lance quipped. He was still very anxious to understand this concept he only knew by name.

"Impressive," said Kevin, "not only did you remember where we left off, but you also tied it to a similar concept from one of my favorite speeches. "The Drum Major Instinct was a homily originally written by J. Wallace and made famous by Dr. Martin Luther King Jr. Keep in mind, that in the sixties, Dr. King's speeches were essentially like the Ted Talks we have today. They were always informative, inspirational, and motivational on one level or another. In this particular speech, Wallace and King basically affirm the idea that everyone wants to be great.

We don't want to simply be in the band; we all have instincts to be the leader or drum major. Furthermore, Wallace and King espouse the notion that there is nothing at all wrong with wanting to be great. However, they challenge the notion of 'how' to be great. In the end (spoiler alert), they assert that the way to greatness is by serving others. Therefore, anyone can be great because anyone can serve. Does that make sense to you Lance?"

“Yes, that sounds like a nice approach to life, but that still doesn’t explain what the Double-Major Instinct is,” Lance replied.

“No, you are right, I am taking the long way to explain this concept,” Kevin continued. “The Drum Major Instinct is the instinct that lies inside all of us to be great. Likewise, the Double-Major Instinct is the instinct to be great at more than one thing.”

But why call it the “Double-Major Instinct?” Lance replied while laughing.

“Good question, I suppose I should eventually answer it right!” They laughed.

“If I told you someone had a university degree in chemistry, university licenses in philosophy and humanities, was a high-school teacher who taught psychology and literature, worked as a lab technician, as well as a night-club bouncer (security) in Buenos Aires and speaks several languages, what would you think the person is? Kevin waited for a reply.

Lance answered bewilderingly, “I literally have no idea what a person with that type of background would be. Is that a real person?” He laughed.

Kevin joined in the laughter, "I just gave you a condensed resume of Pope Francis, the 266th Pope of the Roman Catholic Church! Can you believe it? All of those experiences contributed to his seemingly disconnected passion and dreams of becoming a leader in his religious community. Do you think his other bouncer friends saw him as a pope? Do you think his fellow lab technicians knew about his passion for theology? Do you think Pope Francis himself thought that his scientific pursuits would be a part of his theological pursuits? Either way, it's a fascinating thing to consider, what I refer to as the Double Major Instinct!"

Lance listened to Kevin in amazement at the trivia he had just heard.

"When I was in grade and high school, I was encouraged to engage in a number of different activities: study history, advance literature, and various math courses, to play sports ranging from football, wrestling, baseball, and track. I was invited to and participated in the jazz and symphonic band. In short, the activities were endless. Hence, I developed a variety of skills and excelled in several subjects and extra-curricular activities. However, when I started a university, I was told that I could only choose one major.

Of all the things I had interest in and several things in which I had become proficient, I was told I had to choose one path! When I graduated, I had an opportunity to meet our class valedictorian.

"I talked with her, and we eventually discussed our majors. When I asked her what her major was, she giggled and responded, 'I completed a double-major!' Though she already had my respect and admiration, after hearing what she did, I looked at her as though she was a superhero!"

"Why?" Lance asked.

"Because she had broken through a social-construct that is forced upon us at the university level!" Kevin said passionately. "Can't you see it? A person majors in one area to graduate as an aspiring expert in that field. Once you graduate as an expert, you immediately look for jobs that align with your expertise. We do this because we believe the most earning potential can be achieved in the one area we have studied!"

"Yeah, that's generally the way it works, but there are many people who don't get jobs in their field of study or their major." Lance scowled because he was one of those persons. He recalled the frustration of searching for years without finding an opening in his field.

"But don't you see that life's gift to us is an opportunity to reactivate our Double-Major Instinct?! What was your major?"

"Believe it or not, it was Music Education," replied Lance.

Kevin immediately responded: "But you couldn't find anything in that field, so you eventually entered the world of digital news as a journalist and researcher."

"Yes, that's right."

Kevin continued, "And how long have you been doing this?"

"Approximately eight years."

"So in addition to your degree in music education, you have now amassed eight years of experience and training in digital news for an industry-leading news provider," Kevin declared with pure excitement and passion.

"Yes, yes, so what's thc point?" questioned Lance.

Kevin continued to speak with passion and emphasis, the kind he uses when enlightenment is near.

He stood up and started using objects as he explicated his conclusion.

"Instead of being experienced and educated in only one field, you are now a bonafide expert in two or more different fields! You are essentially in the position of someone who has a Double-Major. Beyond becoming more attractive as an employee, your recently acquired knowledge can serve your dreams as well. One of which was starting your S.T.E.A.M. (Science, Technology Engineering Arts and Math) programming academy for grade-school kids. Who better to write the story for your company about how a small-town boy is returning home to help close the education gap in a tremendous way?"

"How did you know about that?" Lance asked.

"You posted it on social media years ago. We do our research as well," Kevin smiled. "Now imagine using the contacts you have made throughout your career as touch-points to gather support for your efforts."

Lance was beginning to understand Kevin's point. "I could only imagine what type of attention and support I could generate with simply one good story about my school! I really never thought of it that way. I never considered that this detour in life could really lead me back to what I really want to accomplish, but with more experience and resources. Of course, this only works if I decide not to give 'it' up."

Kevin placed his hand on Lance's shoulder and said, "You're exactly right, Lance; once you decide that your perceived setback is only a detour and keep working on your dream, there is no limit to what you can accomplish! The old adage says: 'Don't let people put a period in your life, where there should be a comma.' There should never be a point in life where we are left thinking this is all I will ever be!

There are countless examples of people who decided they were more than their current title at an organization. Just because your title is building engineer, executive assistant, junior sales associate or grill operator doesn't mean that is all you can do. It also doesn't mean that's who you are. You are more than your position in a company, what you made last year or even your last employee evaluation!"

"Yeah, but how do you deal with the managers who only see you for your title and nothing more. They parade around the office as if they are better than us; most of them don't even care about their employees. It's all a big game to them." Lance was clearly reflecting on some of the editors he had worked for in his time at the buinessparody.com home offices.

Kevin replied, “Simple! You have to live like a superhero.”

“Live like a what?” Lance chuckled.

“We will talk about that next week; that’s all the time we have for now,” Kevin responded. “As homework, take a sheet of paper or computer file, and put your name at the top in large letters. Draw a line underneath your name and list the skills you’ve acquired throughout your life at the various jobs you’ve had. You should include both paid jobs and volunteer work, whether it is for a non-profit or a local community theatre, list all of your skills.

Write down all of the titles you’ve held in these various paid or volunteer jobs. Make sure you have the latest verbiage for that particular field and note all the positions you have held. While listing those skills, also list the duties you have performed throughout the years.

“Once you have finished, think about and analyze how each of those skills could contribute to the dream you are working on. If it’s starting a company, ask yourself how these skills can help you build your brand. If it’s a particular career, see how those skills might allow you to be hired for a position a few levels below or close to an organization in your desired field.

Finally, see if you can include those skills in various resumé templates for jobs you are considering.”

Actions & Endnotes

Remember Lance's Homework:

1. Take a sheet of paper or computer file and put your name at the top in large letters. Now, draw a line underneath your name and list the skills you've acquired throughout your life at the various jobs you've had. You should include both paid jobs, hobbies and volunteer work, whether it be for a non-profit, or a local community theatre, list all your skills.
2. List all the titles you've held in these various paid or volunteer jobs. Make sure you have the latest verbiage for that particular field and make a note of all the positions you have held.
3. While listing those skills, also list the duties and certifications that you have performed throughout the years.

4. Once you have finished, think about and analyze how each of those skills could contribute to the dream you are working on. If it's starting a company, ask, how can these skills help me to build my brand? If it's a career, see how those skills might allow you to be hired for a position a few levels below, or close to an organization in your desired field. Finally, see if you can include those skills in various resume' templates for jobs you are considering.
5. If you are not impressed by what you see, it's okay; this is NOT how you finish, this is a skills inventory for where you are now.

   The grind is a part of the process:

   - Look at your job like paid on the job training for your dream
   - What skills have I learned that transfer to my dream
   - What relationships can I leverage to contribute to my dream / destiny
   - What monetary benefits can I leverage toward my dream. (i.e. investing to start business, increasing earning power and saving towards your dream, saving up to become financially independent to pursue your dream)

4

Live Like A Superhero

Lance thought about his last conversation with Kevin every day. Even though he was an admitted skeptic and analytical to a fault, he couldn't shake the feeling of liberty and inspiration he felt in their last meeting. He knew Kevin was a great speaker and definitely had unmistakable charisma, but what he felt seemed to come from more than that. It was empowering to know he had options in his life; this wasn't a "dead-end" job, and if he had a master plan, everything in life could fit into it. *Live like a superhero, huh*, Lance said to himself. *This ought to be interesting*. He had to admit while all these ideas sounded like t-shirt slogans, the truths they illustrated were definitely impactful. He finished his assignment and could barely sleep before his next meeting with Kevin. He spent the entire week working on his homework. Lance was surprised to see how much he had forgotten about his life and previous jobs.

"Good Morning, Ashley," Lance greeted her as he entered the suite.

"Good Morning, Lance! He's ready whenever you are," Ashley said as she exited Kevin's office.

"Great!" Lance responded and headed toward the office.

“Lance, how are you this morning? Have you thought about our last conversation? Did you complete your homework?” Kevin asked, as Lance unzipped his bag in the office.

“Homework is right here!” Lance said with a smile that was beaming with pride.

“Lance, that is terrific! You should be proud of yourself because now, you are taking control of your life and configuring your master plan.

Lance thought about it for a moment. He concluded that the answer might be obvious, but he should ask instead of assume. Then he went on to ask, “What is a master plan?”

“That’s a great question!” Kevin responded with excitement. “One of my favorite definitions of a master plan comes from the International Bank for Reconstruction and Development (IBRD), which is a subsidiary of the World Bank Group. The organization defines a master plan as a dynamic long-term planning document that provides a conceptual layout to guide future growth and development."

Kevin stared at Lance for a moment, hoping he would make the connection. "Get it? Long-term but dynamic plan for future growth and development! Many people think planning is the lock-box discipline of laying out a strategy and sticking with it no matter what changes may occur, but as we often discover, life is not always that predictable. We can't become unhinged when things don't work according to the plan. In fact, a real master plan is able to change, be dynamic, and still remain focused on the long-term goal. It won't always work out HOW we planned it, but a good master plan can always work out the WHAT we planned! Don't let the HOW cause you to lose focus on the WHAT. Stay focused on the master plan, and allow it to encompass all the changes that life's challenges can bring."

So, this we—"

"Live like a superhero!" Lanced interrupted.

"Okay, okay, you remembered," Kevin said with nervous laughter

"So, what does it mean to live like a superhero? What does the illustration mean?" Lance asked as he sat down in front of Kevin's desk.

"First, you'll have to forgive me. I may veer off in this conversation because it is about one of my favorite subjects: superheroes! Ha-ha!" Kevin continued: "When I mention the word 'superhero,' I am referring to a specific kind. Over the last few years, we have witnessed the birth of Marvel Cinematic Studios. Many people immediately think about characters like Iron Man, the Hulk, Thor, and Captain America when you say superheroes. Make no mistake about it; those are some of my favorite characters."

Lance could clearly see that from the large Iron Man watch Kevin wore quite often. It was hard to miss!

Kevin continued: "But when I use the phrase superheroes, I am referring to a more old-school version of superheroes: characters like Superman or my favorite Batman! One of the main differences between these characters and some of the aforementioned Marvel heroes is that Superman and Batman both have secret identities. While in the Marvel Cinematic Universe, their heroes are known by the entire world. On the DC Comics side, many of their main characters have secret identities. Do you see where I am going with this?"

"I think so. Are you saying you need to have a secret identity?" Lance stammered,

"Yes, in a way, that is exactly what I am saying! Most of the time, these heroes had secret identities to protect friends and family. In one iteration of Batman, his secret identity, Billionaire Bruce Wayne, is known as a billionaire playboy. As a result, their identities were often the complete opposite of their hero personages. Therefore, Bruce Wayne's personality was the complete opposite of Batman. Bruce played his role so well it removed all suspicion he could be the Batman. And Batman played his role so well it removed any suspicion he could be Bruce Wayne. Again, this was something done to protect friends and family. But Bruce Wayne embraced these challenges because he was committed to fulfilling his purpose as Batman. Bruce would tolerate being called an irresponsible, spoiled, rich orphan to protect his life as Batman. Likewise, we have to be willing to lead double lives in pursuit of our passions." Kevin paused to see if Lance would capture the concept his story illustrated.

"So like Batman, oh I mean Bruce, we should play both of our roles so well, no one would suspect the other role exists," Lance replied.

"Perfectly adapted and understood! We have to be the perfect Batman and Bruce Wayne. That means working a little harder to ensure we can maintain our proficiencies in two different areas. It means we have to continue learning, training, and networking in two different fields."

Kevin continued: "The challenges of living like a superhero are many. I recall listening to an interview with the famous musical artist John Legend. He mentioned when he started working on larger budget musical projects, he was also working during the day as a management consultant. He would spend late nights in the studio and doing local shows. But in the daytime, he was Bruce Wayne, going to work and performing at his job. In the end, he was eventually awarded a major label contract. Actually, he became one of the youngest people to achieve an EGOT (winning an Emmy, Grammy, Oscar, and Toney awards)."

"Live like a superhero. Well, it sounds like I have some work to do," Lance said.

"Don't we all! And remember, your day job may be necessary for now, but make sure you save time to pursue your passions. A farmhand was caught by his wife working in the middle of the night. His wife asked him, 'Why are you working here after working the entire day in their fields?' His response was: 'I'm not going to spend all day working their fields without taking the time to plow my own!'"

Lance nodded in agreement as Kevin continued, "Remember take the time and work your fields. Live like a superhero and pursue your passion!"

Actions & Endnotes

Atlanta Falcons GM Thomas Dimitroff started working in the NFL as a groundskeeper. While he was a groundskeeper in Cleveland, the head coach of the Browns was Bill Belicheck. Thomas Dimitroff worked as a groundskeeper during the day and returned at night to attend coaching and scouting meetings. In these meetings he learned how to scout players for an NFL team. In his very first year as an NFL GM, Thomas won the coveted award of NFL Executive of the year 2009.

- Identify resources that can provide training for your passion, or opportunities for you to practice whatever your passion is. You would be surprised what companies; people will allow you to do for them if you are working for free. The idea is to maximize the opportunity by learning.

- YouTube is quickly becoming a great source for training on all types of things. Many companies and accomplished entrepreneurs have channels that you can subscribe to and learn some information about your industry. If its music, find your instrument on YouTube. If its video editing, check out sites like Lynda.com and LinkedIn Learning to find the latest trainings in those fields. If its stand-up comedy, develop partnerships with local clubs and learn about the amateur hour. If it is legal work, visit the court room and volunteer for public defenders, or have a meeting with the District Attorney (they work for you) and get advice on how to get started.
- Bottom Line: Find opportunities for training and practice of your passion. Build your skills to become an asset in whatever your field may be.

5

Superpowers: Learnability & Relatability

Lance kept thinking about what Kevin said: *live like a superhero.* Eventually, Lance replied, "It's funny you mentioned you have to live like a superhero! But we all know that illustration has its limits. I mean, if we are superheroes what are our superpowers?"

"Your skepticism never ceases to amaze me!" replied Kevin with a chuckle.

"What? I'm serious. You just said we have to live like superheroes if we are going to work our dreams. So, what are our superpowers? What are yours?" asked Lance.

Kevin sat back in his chair laughing again: "I suppose we all have the same superpowers. They are available to all those who are willing to go beyond the status quo and hang on to their passions. They are equally important and irreplaceable. Pursuing your dreams will require learnability and relatability!"

"Okay, I'm interested. How does it work?" answered Lance.

At this point, Ashley had briefly entered the office to leave something on Kevin's desk. On her way out, Kevin asked, "Ashley, what is the name of the author I have been raving about with the quote about learning?"

Almost instantly, Ashley answered, "Alvin

Toffler!"

"That's it!" Kevin exclaimed.

While Lance made a mental note that if he ever made it on a game show and could choose a partner, Ashley was definitely the right move.

"'The illiterate of the 21st century will not be those who cannot read and write, but those who cannot learn, unlearn, and relearn' (Alvin Toffler). Meaning, our ability to learn will determine the extent of our success in many areas. Beyond it being a brilliant statement, it is so very true," said Kevin.

"You know what? That is certainly true in relationships. If you don't eventually learn what makes your partner happy or angry, the relationship will not survive for any extended period of time." Lance had just gone through a breakup; that was the first illustration he could think of.

As an award pause filled the room, Kevin thought, *wow! This guy is really a different bird.* Nevertheless, Kevin stammered into his answer, "U-U-Uh, y-y-yeah, okay… I suppose that works. I was thinking more along the lines of companies that hire people based on their belief that the person can learn the intricacies of the job as it is performed in the company's context. While their prior skills, education or experience certainly factor into that belief, it is ultimately the employees' ability to learn their new role that will determine their success. In short, learning is the bridge to wherever you need to go. In fact, there is a statement I live by: 'I don't know everything, but I can learn anything!' That is your superpower when multitasking in the world of job, dreams, and careers."

"You can learn anything?!" Lance said in his usual skeptical and somewhat facetious tone.

"That's right. With the proper motivation, time, and instruction / resources I can learn anything. And you can learn it as well. For example, if I tell you I have a position in my company, but I can't find anyone to fill this position, however, since I like you, I am going to hire you to do it, provide training for the position so you will understand how to do your job, and give you about three months to learn how to be successful in this position, what would you say?"

"I would ask what the job pays," Lance said quickly.

"Approximately 2.5 million dollars a ye—"

"Yes, yes I would! Where do I need to sign?"

Lance interjected.

"It was a hypothetical question, genius, and your time is up! Mr. Seinfeld has a 3 p.m. appointment."

"Thank you, Ashley! And yes, that was a hypothetical scenario, but do you see the point? You can learn anything with the right resources, motivation, and time," said Kevin.

Lance thought about his new superpower – how he had used it before and how he could use it again. He had never thought about the ability to learn something as an asset. While still packing up for the day he contemplated the preface of their conversation and asked: "Didn't you say we have two superpowers? What is the other one?"

Ashley stood at the door waiting to usher Lance out of Kevin's office. However, she noticed the compassion in Kevin's eyes. She knew he would need more time to reply to the "genius" who was now delaying the entire schedule for the day. Knowing where this was going, she exhaustingly replied, "I'll tell them you are running ten minutes behind schedule, sir!" And then on her way out of the office she whispered, "Some people just don't know when to quit."

"Relatability! Every time I think about it, I recall

an old sitcom I used to watch. On that show, the psychologist was giving advice to a client about how to deal with some rather complex feelings at a very interpersonal family gathering. The advice was to relax, relate, release," Kevin replied with an executive giggle.

"Nevertheless, the second point in my advice and that of the psychologist is the same. Relating or relatability is your second superpower. There is a saying that 'Everything you need is in a relationship.' You may be more familiar with the adage: 'It's who you know not what you know.' I truly misunderstood this statement for years, and it is especially misunderstood in a social-media-driven society where people mistake knowing a name for knowing a person. We sometimes feel tweeting at people and adding them as friends on Facebook or LinkedIn are the same as getting to know people. Unfortunately, the aforementioned activities can't substitute for actual relationship with people.

"To be clear, building relationships with people isn't for the purpose of using them. If that were the case, you would only need to relate to people who could help you. Many people attempt to manage relationships this way. However, life is unpredictable, and you can easily miscalculate or diagnose 'who' can help you by presuming you are on a higher or greater level than someone else. Don't be that person because levels are fluid, socially-engineered structures and akin to the concept of house appraisals. Your home may be worth millions today but worth hundreds tomorrow, all depending on the social-economic illusion of goods and services. Like a home's value, we can't tell who might be able to help us or when they can do it."

"So I should be nice to everyone!" Lance exclaimed.

"Yeah, that's the general point here."

"That could be exhausting. I mean, always smiling, helpful, and caring to everyone."

"Everyone that you can! Being kind, relatable or nice is the simplest and most inexpensive investment with the most return. And you are investing in the most precious resource in the market: people! It doesn't cost anything to be kind, but it can cost you everything when you are not."

Kevin went on to say, "This concept is so important for one single and most important reason. When you are kind and relatable to people, it prevents you from using people in situations where they can help you!"

"What do you mean, using them?" asked Lance.

"I mean, taking advantage of people's influence or ability solely for your own advancement, without care for their well-being."

Lance immediately thought of times when he had been used. How he had helped Veronica in the weeks leading up to her interview, putting her information together and gathering research. However, after she was awarded the job, she never really spoke to him again. He also recalled how he had used a person to get a lead on the product launch story some years ago. He thought about how when that employee was reprimanded for helping him, he didn't do anything to help. He never spoke to the person again because he had achieved what he desired.

"I imagine you are thinking about times when you used people or people used you. But I want to challenge you, don't just recall the events; think about the feelings associated with those events. There was a time this topic would always leave me angry or sad. Now, this topic makes me glad that I am better at relating to people because *all* people matter. In truth, we all have the same creator."

"Hey, I remember something you said in an interview last year along those same lines. I actually have it in my bag. It was part of my research for today's meeting. I found it!

"You said: 'With the advancement and growth of knowledge, we have so many more divisions in our society. Racism was a major point of division in early American history. But now, there are so many more -isms! And every -ism is another point of division. The reality is we are all the same race, same creator, but we face many different challenges. However, our challenges should not define us; our differences should not be our identities, and the place for understanding and unity starts with commonality, not division.' I always thought that was a radically different perspective from our general approach. But you mean to tell me that ideology is what drives you to be kind and relatable?" asked Lance.

"Eureka! Believing that all men and women are created equal can be the impetus for being kind and relatable. And relatability is your (equally) greatest superpower! Learn to be relatable. Let me give you an example," Kevin continued. "About ten years ago, a friend of mine worked for a small business that sponsored a conference for business leaders. They brought in a world-renowned speaker. Naturally, they took care of all the logistics regarding hotel and airfare. But at the last moment, the driver for the speaker called out sick. When the issue came to the attention of leadership, no one in the room wanted to fill in for the driver. My friend Travis volunteered and went to pick up the speaker from the airport. He drove around the speaker for the entire weekend and used his relatability to build a bond with this world-renowned speaker. About a year later, the speaker, he drove around, offered him a job paying nearly three times what he made working for his current company. Simply because he was relatable and willing to serve, he created another opportunity for himself."

Actions & Endnotes

The Power of Learning

1. Once something is learned, you should work to understand HOW it can be retained. How can I remember what I learned and continue to work on my skills?

Adult Learning Retention Statistics:

Lecture – 5%
Reading – 10%
Demonstration – 30%
Group – 50%
Practice and Doing (experiential!) – 75%!

(Stats from ASTD American Society for Training and Development)

Once you learn it, practice it, use it! Even if it is done for gratis, the payment is your ability to further your learning! Example: If you are a photographer, offer to take pictures for a cheaper rate, so that you use the photos to build your portfolio.

2. The ability to learn is the NEW literacy, without it, one becomes obsolete in the world of Human Resources. You will always be useful if you can learn.

3. Remember: You don't know everything, but you can learn anything! (If someone paid you 20 million dollars to learn the fundamentals of rocket science, you would learn it immediately) learning flows better with motivation. Therefore, keep your "Why" in our heart and mind.

6

Their Employee = Your Brand

Lance left Kevin's office grateful for the time, but contemplative about everything they had discussed. He found himself spending less time on social media because he was taking some time to reflect and clarify his thoughts about all the conversations they had. *If you don't work on your dream, it becomes a nightmare.* Lance remembered and thought to himself, *You have to be willing to live like a superhero or work like an entrepreneur – around the clock – to invest the appropriate time in your venture. You must be willing to learn and to stay current on your craft or skillset, so you will be ready for your opportunity*. Maybe Kevin did know what he was talking about. Perhaps it wasn't a matter of luck as much as it was being prepared for the opportunity. *Of course, that's the reason one should never give up*. Lance continued to rehearse these thoughts to himself.

That night, he pulled out an old project from college that required him to visualize where he would be in ten, fifteen, and twenty years. Laughing to himself, he thought, *I'm so far off-track from where I wanted to be at this age in my life. I was so focused when I was younger. I had dreams and visions about how I could make the world a better place. But now, work, kids, life, all these things make it impossible to have that type of focus. No, no! I have to remain focused and keep my eyes on the prize. That's how I got off track the last time.* Lance argued with himself.

The more he thought about it, the more he questioned whether he could do it. *Is it possible to still hang on to a dream and deal with the realities of life? Who wants to pursue a dream that will never manifest? It's like dangling a piece of fruit just out of the reach of a man who is starving to death. Won't it be even more tormenting to hope, work, and wish for a dream that doesn't come to fruition*? But then, Lance thought about why he was miserable at work, the real reason he hated to drag himself into the office. He thought about Kevin's words to him, "Not understanding 'What's This For' makes work excruciating."

Lance was tired of wasting life by not enjoying it. *If I only enjoy one hundred and four days out of the year, and enjoyment on those days is completely dependent on the weather, that means I spend the other two hundred and sixty-one days trying to get to the weekends. In other words, I would be wasting 2,610 days over the next ten years. That's almost the total number of days I have wasted over the last seven years.* Then Lance said aloud, "I don't want to live that way! That's much more difficult than working and enjoying the journey towards my dreams."

He looked at Kevin's number and verbalized his internal consternation. "He gave me permission to use it. There is no point in having his number if I am not going to dial it at some point. But it is somewhat late for a personal call. What time does he go to bed anyway? Maybe I should just text him; that's less intrusive. But what if he doesn't see it until much later than now?" Lance sighed, "I'll just take my chances and call."

"Kevin, hello Kevin? " Lance nervously asked.

"Hello Lance, how are you? Having a good evening?"

Lance was so relieved Kevin wasn't angry at being disturbed.

"I've been thinking about all the advice you gave regarding the pursuit of my dream and not giving up on my passions while adding skills and becoming more proficient in other areas. But I am having trouble with one more part of this..." Lance paused to transpose his thoughts into words.

"Go ahead Lance, I'm listening friend," Kevin reassured.

"What happens when we get jobs that are completely off the radar of what we are proficient in, passionate about or even skilled at? I mean, I had to do some things just because it paid more; it allowed me to stay home more for any number of practical reasons."

Lance blurted out: "The career I am in now has gone from a one-year bridge job to a six to seven-year detour. I've been here so long; I don't know if I could imagine an exit strategy to get back on course with my dreams and passion.

"I have not found a position in our company that is even remotely related to what I would like to do in education and the arts. How did you handle it when your main job was driving for Uber, but you still had a desire to be a hospitality industry magnate? How do you make sure you don't get trapped in the matrix of work, annual objectives, PMP, and repeat?"

Kevin, as always, took time to understand what Lance was really asking. He had a way of listening to the question to answer or address the real impetus behind the request. "First Lance, that is a great question. Over the last few days and weeks, we've discussed what some people have to work their dream, but it seems like you are asking about how these people didn't get caught in the web of complacency. I can't speak for any of them, but I will share insight from my story.

"One of the most popular philosophic theories about jobs, in the sense of economic philosophy, is that jobs are created as a result of problems or needs. When a company or organization has a problem: too many orders being placed in a day, for example, they create a job to resolve that issue. 'Let's hire more order fulfillment personnel.'

"The word 'employ,' is derived from the Latin word *implicare,* which in the 15th century meant 'to enfold' – *Im* meaning within or in and *plicare* "to fold." By definition, an employee is someone enveloped or enfolded within the company to solve its challenges and problems. And that is exactly what being employed can feel like. It can feel as if you are being swallowed up, maybe even suffocated by the company or the problems you were hired to solve. This can be really great when the company is dedicated to employee development, loyalty, and has a culture that supports this type of harmonious balance between employee and company. However, everyone doesn't have an opportunity to work in this type of environment. This is the situation I found myself in some years ago.

"I was enfolded in a company that had a poor work culture, treated people badly, and did very little to develop its employees. I had two options, blend in and continue to be enfolded within that culture or stay connected to my dream and treat this employment stop as a bridge. I made the decision that day, not to ever be an employee but to recognize my name, work, and reputation as my personal brand!"

"Wow," Lance responded, "I never thought about that."

Kevin continued, "On one particular occasion, I was going above and beyond for our customers. I was following up on service issues and doing things that weren't in my job description. One day, a manager called me into his office; you will never guess what he said."

Lanced laughed and responded, "I know your luck. He probably gave you a ten-thousand-dollar bonus as they did at the end of one of the Undercover Boss television episodes!"

The two shared a laugh and Kevin continued, "I wish! He brought me into his office and said these words: I see your performance and how you are getting things done really fast. I notice the customers are pleased with how you follow up to ensure their incorrect parts have been replaced. I just want you to know, it doesn't matter."

"Excuse me," I replied.

He continued talking. "What you are doing doesn't matter. You're not going to get a raise; no one is going to care either way, and you are certainly not getting my job, so just calm down and blend in with everyone else."

"He said what?" Lance was shocked at what he heard.

"Yeah, that was his response to my extra effort," Kevin replied.

"And what did you do?" Lance asked.

"I politely thanked him for his advice and told him that was the only way I knew how to work. I don't consider myself an employee. I consider myself a brand. And whoever decides to hire me, this is the type of effort I am going to give. It was demotivating for a moment, but then I realized while that type of effort was not appreciated there, this was the brand I was building, and it had very little to do with them. Within three months, another opportunity was created by my decision to continue going above and beyond. And the punchline is I was eventually hired by one of their customers!"

"I can only imagine that guy's response when you called him to see why an order was not correct!" Lance laughed.

"It did take him a while to get accustomed to that." They shared another laugh.

Then Kevin, in a very sincere tone, continued, "Lance, I want you to understand, you are never trapped anywhere. If you are willing to learn and work, there is literally nothing that can stop you! The opportunities are endless for people who know how to represent and protect their brand. Yes, ensure you do a great job at work, get a great mid and end-of-year review and when you leave, get a reference letter because all of those things become testimonials of your brand. They will see you as a great employee; however, beyond the context of that position and company, they will see you as a great brand!"

Lance nodded his head in agreement. While Kevin couldn't see him, he could feel that a connection was made.

"Inevitably, things will happen that are beyond our control. Eventually, everyone has an opportunity to make a choice. The options may not be great, but the choice is still ours. Make the choice that will give you better options the next time you have to choose. I chose to continue building my brand in spite of the context in which I worked and so can you. Think about this, Lance. What is the quintessential element of everyone's dream, no matter what it may be? What is the element that is going to be present in everyone's pursuit of their master plan?"

Lance thought about the riddle for a brief moment and then Kevin responded, "You! Everyone's dream includes them. It requires you in some way shape or form. Building your brand increases the value of the most important part of your dream and that's you (the dreamer)."

"Well, Lance, it's been a pleasure. Don't we have another appointment next week?" Kevin interjected on the contemplative silence. "I will have Ashley email you about the next meeting's time and place."

"Yes, we do," replied Lance. "Thank you so much for taking my call tonight! Enjoy what is left of it."

Lance hung up. While running to get his iPad, he thought to himself, *I'm a brand, a business entity, not an employee. I must write that down!*

Actions & Endnotes

Think of places in which your brand is advertised. LinkedIn, Instagram, Twitter, Facebook, and other Social Media. Is it updated? Does it represent you? Is it a good representation of all your skills? Is it a good representation of you? Is there anything you wouldn't want an employer to see? Be conservative in Social Media use. When you feel very strongly about something, use discretion in sharing it. Do your best not to offend people. Most importantly, if someone has angered you, go and talk to them, don't argue and fight on the world wide web! This is YOUR brand!

7

Balancing Pursuit and Completion

"Finally, an out of town trip!" Lance rejoiced as he reviewed an email from Ashley with and itinerary for his final meeting with Kevin.

"Okay, okay, where are we going?" Lance muttered as he skimmed through the email looking for his destination details.

"Flight booked for Atlanta, GA! Perfect!" Lance was excited as he knew the spring arrived on time in the south, as opposed to what happens in the north. "Warmer climate, here I come!"

"Jennifer, I will see you in a few days – meeting with Seinfeld in Atlanta tomorrow!" Lance announced as he walked by her office.

"Wait, wait, before you leave! I don't remember seeing a travel request for this trip or did I misplace it?" Jennifer questioned.

"No, there wasn't a travel request, Mr. Seinfeld is actually covering the trip for me," Lance said with a humble sense of accomplishment.

"Wow, you two must have really made a connection! Awesome work! I can't wait to read the interview. I know it's going to be good. Travel safely! And wish Mildred a happy birthday on your way out. You won't be here tomorrow. Just say it now, so you won't forget!" Jennifer advised.

"I will and thanks for the opportunity again," Lance said while leaving.

Jennifer could tell Lance was happy and excited, but she didn't know if it was because of the travel or that he and Kevin were connecting so well. At any rate, she was happy to see him happy for a change. "Happy Birthday, Mildred," she heard Lance yelling on his way out of the office. Jennifer was surprised and thought to herself, *he remembered*! She had figured with all of his excitement that he would have forgotten.

On arrival in Atlanta, Ga., Lance checked into the hotel and found Ashley in the lobby. *Now is the time to make my move. I can make this trip a two-for-one*. Lance imagined the possibilities. He walked over to Ashley and was surprised at her response.

"Lance! I was waiting for you," she said.

"You were?" replied Lance.

"Yes, I wanted to give you this ticket for the meeting tomorrow."

At this point, Lance was so disoriented he couldn't get his pick-up game face together.

"Wait, what do I need a ticket for?" Lance responded in a bewildered tone.

"Mr. Seinfeld said he would do his final session with you at tomorrow's game," Ashley replied in a matter of fact tone.

"A game, what…" Lance started opening the envelope, "Oh, the baseball game – got it. We're going to the Braves game." Lance was relieved to no longer be in the dark about tomorrow's itinerary.

"I'm glad you figured it out, but you also could have let me finish my sentence to understand that much faster! Mr. Seinfeld is on a flight for tomorrow morning, so we'll meet for breakfast." Ashley replied while walking away with a flirtatious smile.

"Wait, please wait, one more thing!" Lance raised his voice in the lobby.

"See you tomorrow, Lance," Ashley said as she continued walking away. She already knew what Lance wanted to ask and figured she would save him the embarrassment of declining his invitation.

Right, thanks again. Guess I'll have to try again tomorrow, Lance said to himself.

Lance ate dinner in the hotel lobby and made some edits to his interview notes from earlier sessions. He kept wondering what the final lesson in this session would be. *It seems like we covered everything you would need. Maybe this is just a session to have some fun.*

In many ways, Lance had already started putting into practice what he learned from their previous conversations. He was more motivated and inspired than he had ever been about continuing to work his dream and his job. But he couldn't help the analytical part of his mind. It was racing, probing and trying to figure out what the next lesson might be.

When the next day arrived, Lance got ready, grabbed his ticket and headed down to the lobby to meet Mr. Seinfeld for brunch.

"Lance, I'm glad you could make it! Did you sleep well last night?" Kevin said with his usual enthusiasm.

"I slept well, thank you and thanks for allowing me to come on the trip. I am looking forward to the game today!" Lance said as he sat down for breakfast.

"Indeed, so am I! We have a couple of stops to make first and then we are going to enjoy a 'businessman special.' That's what the baseball world refers to as an early noon start time."

The two finished breakfast, and Ashley arrived with the driver to take them to their first appointment. Their first stop was a quick visit to the Atlanta office of Kevin's financial advisor. While Lance was not in the meeting, he noticed the two gentlemen were having a very pleasant conversation. Lance thought about how it would feel to one day have the type of money to have pleasant conversations about.

"How was brunch this morning?" Ashley asked Lance as he attempted to lip-read the conversation between Kevin and his advisor.

"Brunch was fine; thank you for asking. But do you know why we are here?" Lance asked while still staring at the lips of the two gentlemen in the office.

"Mr. Seinfeld would have to tell you why we are here, if he chooses. I do know why we are not here. We are not here to try and listen to confidential conversations," Ashley said as she commanded his attention with her smile, tone, and professionalism.

"I'm sorry; you are right. I used to work in the investigative wing of the company; sometimes it's hard to turn it off." Just as Lance realized he was alone with Ashley again and could resume gathering the courage and words to ask her out, Kevin's meeting concluded. Kevin and his financial advisor shook hands and hugged. *I'd hug the guy and more if I had made millions by managing his millions,* Lance thought to himself.

"Is everyone ready? We are off to the stadium." It was at this point that Lance realized Kevin was still very overdressed to attend a baseball game in the middle of the day.

"Are you going to change clothes?" Lance remarked.

"Not yet, I have one more meeting at the stadium and then I'll probably change there," Kevin replied as he opened the door for Ashley and Lance to proceed to the car.

When they arrived at the stadium, the driver parked in the front and let Kevin know he would be in the area if he needed anything else during the game. Immediately, the stadium staff asked to see the tickets. Lance was blown away when he discovered the section, they would be seated in. *In the suites!* Fantastic! *Okay, okay, let me calm down and comport myself like a professional. I've been there before.* Lance repeated this to himself like a meditation mantra.

The business trio entered the large, luxurious suite to find a small collection of people who were expecting Kevin. They all greeted him as though he were their best friend. Most of Kevin's interactions were exactly like that: pleasant, day-altering encounters. Ashley and Lance were again ushered to another area of the suite where the players warming up could be observed. The suite staff was very friendly and attentive. They served them refreshments even before they asked.

While Lance realized he was once again alone with Ashley, he could tell the timing was definitely bad. When she wasn't staring in the direction of Kevin's meeting, clasping her hands as if she was hoping for something, she was looking at some of the more physically endowed world-class athletes on the field. It didn't take much for the former investigative reporter to see the difference between his physique and some of the players who were holding Ashley's attention. *I'll just wait for a better time,* Lance concluded.

Once again, the meeting ended with a bunch of handshakes and hugs. It also finished just in time for the game to start. Ashley immediately walked over and asked if there was anything Kevin needed. At his request, she pulled out several envelopes for each attendee at the meeting. As she handed them out, small cheers erupted in the suite as they realized these were gift cards to one of Kevin's restaurants.

Once again reunited, the trio headed to their area of the suite, while Ashley requested the bag for Kevin's wardrobe change be brought over. Kevin went into the men's washroom and changed almost as fast as a certain superhero who changed back into his secret identity as a reporter for the iconic "Daily Planet!"

The three sat down as the game had already started. Ashley could barely wait to get to this moment. With the most passion and anticipation Lance had ever heard from Ashley, she asked, "Did we get it? Are you in?"

Kevin laughed and said, "Wow, could you let me get a sip of my drink first?"

"Come on. You know I am dying to find out. All those reports I had to run, all the numbers I had to check, I have to know how this worked out!" Ashley pleaded.

"You are right; your work was invaluable in getting us to this point. I'm really sorry to report; we didn't get it," Kevin said in a most disappointed tone.

"Get what? What's happening?" Lance asked.

"The group over there is a collection of owners for the team. My meeting was to try to procure a minority stake in the team. Unfortunately, we are a little short of the capital needed to secure the entire share, so I'll have to wait another time. Anyway, let's get ready to watch a great game!"

After allowing a few minutes to digest the news or the lack thereof, Lance thought about how close he came to breaking news for his company. He thought about how it would feel to be the reporter on the scene. "Doesn't it bother you that you just lost a tremendous multi-million dollar investment? And after all the success you achieved in the hospitality industry, why are you attempting to get into the sports industry? I thought hospitality and the restaurant business were your dream."

Kevin positioned himself so he could coach a very disappointed Ashley and a more-than-inquisitive reporter Lance.

"Guys, we are in pursuit of something that is only complete when our lives end. It's similar to the proverbial 'life-long school of learning.' You never stop attempting to be better and achieve the next level of success. Don't allow complacency to rob you of something you couldn't even dream of. The truth is our dreams are only the seed of a proverbial destiny forest. It is a guideline to get you on a level you could not imagine or dream of while you were on your previous level. Our Dreams are like intersections or meeting points for where life really begins. You'll find that your dream will truly lead you to places and things above all you could ask or think. That's the tragedy of not pursuing your dream. The dream is simply the springboard for where your life takes off. Once I achieved my dream of independent wealth in the hospitality industry, it opened other opportunities for me in areas I would never have thought to look – like the billion-dollar sports industry. So, this set back isn't defeat; it's a benchmark on a journey that will be completed hopefully many, many years from now."

After a brief pause, Kevin went on to say, "I fulfilled my purpose, which was to come here and try. Now, I am going to enjoy a baseball game, and you should both do the same. Listen, living this kind of life, you will always feel as if you are behind because we are envisioning the next success and the next level of that success. At one point in my life, I would become depressed because I didn't achieve the goals I planned. I got so depressed that I stopped trying to achieve the goals. I didn't want to work on them because I feared being disappointed again. But then I learned disappointment is a test for you and me."

Lance felt one of those eye-opening moments happening. He thought to himself, *this is the lesson he brought me along to learn.*

Kevin continued, "The word disappointed means to fail to meet an expectation or hope. But the word "disappointed" is derived from the Middle English word *disapointen, which means* to dispossess or disown. So, every word has an etymology that, in some cases, inextricably binds the word to its original meaning and use. That's the test of disappointment! It is to attempt to have us dispossess our hopes and our dreams! Don't stay in disappointment for too long. Decide to hold on to hope, even though you have a set-back, break-up, mistake, layoff, termination, bad grades, letters of rejection, investors that don't see the plan or whatever bad news you face. Don't dispossess your dream. Don't fall into the trap of disappointment."

Kevin continued in a most solemn and sober tone: "Many people decide that the numbness of having no hope is better than having disappointment. But regret is the slowest, most potent, poison in the world. It works slowly, but if you live long enough to be infected, the burning pain of 'I wish' dwarfs the pain of disappointment in infinitely more excruciating ways. Well, enough of that. We've got base runners at the bottom of the first here." Kevin shifted the conversation again.

Lance and Ashley nodded at each other realizing they were not only hearing a lesson, but they were watching one as well. As the game progressed, around the fourth innings, one of the interns from the earlier meeting came over to Ashley and mentioned she should have the email by now.

Kevin stopped the young man and said: "Wait, I thought we were kidding. Is that really an offer?"

The young man responded with a wink, "The details are in the email, Mr. Seinfeld."

"How about that?" Kevin responded in humorous disbelief.

"What?" responded both Lance and Ashley. Naturally, Ashley was checking her email for his message.

"Well, in the meeting, one of the owners remarked that I could open a location for my restaurant in a new sector of the stadium. All proceeds would go towards reaching the threshold for the number of shares I need to purchase from the team. I certainly thought it was a great idea. I am just shocked they were seriously considering it. It looks as though by next season, we'll have permanent access to the owner's suite," Kevin said as Ashley literally jumped up and down in excitement! She immediately called Mrs. Seinfeld to tell her the news.

Lance, clearly emotionally overloaded to a point of disbelief realized he had breaking news about Seinfeld's restaurant conglomerate! He imagined how happy his boss would be to find out they were breaking this story. Kevin laughed and pointed toward the sky in a joyous motion.

"Last question, off the record," Lance said while dialing Jennifer his editor. "You said we would have access to the owner's suite moving forward. I'm not your employee."

Kevin placed his hand on his shoulder. "You are a friend, and after all of our time and conversations, I am invested in your success. We now have a relationship! I guess your superpowers do work after all. Now, just don't give up on your dream. You never know where it will take you from here."

###

Connect with us on social media and join the conversation of jobs and dreams:

- Worklikeasuperhero@instagram
- *Keeping Your Day Job and Your Day Dream* on Facebook/worklikeasuperhero@facebook.com
- Worklikeasuperhero@twitter.com

For bookings, please send an email to: bookinginquiry@kbryant2.com.

Note: If you enjoyed the book, check out the soundtrack: "Keeping My Day Job and My Day Dream" on iTunes and everywhere digital music is sold.

About the Author

Kenneth Bryant II is a native of Decatur, Georgia, located in metro-Atlanta. He graduated from Southwest DeKalb High School and went on to obtain a bachelor's degree from Beulah Heights University. He has also completed masters-level degrees in both Secondary Education (M.Ed.) and Christian Studies (M.A.) at Grand Canyon University.

His life and work experiences have allowed him to be conversant in several fields, and serve in numerous positions, such as: Serial Entrepreneur and Visionary, Fortune 500 Learning & Development Director, Executive Trainer, Motivational Speaker, Published Author, S.E.S.A.C. Music Publisher and Song Writer, Musician, Minister, High School Teacher, Leadership Coach and many other roles.

Motivated by a genuine desire to help people fulfill purpose in their lives, he has served in various contexts to awaken, develop, and grow a desire in others to maximize their potential. His varied experiences and skills have allowed him to interface and collaborate with leaders from various industries, all while maintaining the focus to cultivate a movement that encourages people to live each day with hope for reaching their dreams.

You may contact Kenneth Bryant II using the information provided below.

Kenneth Bryant II
kbryant2.org
LinkedIn: Kenneth Bryant II

Printed in the USA
CPSIA information can be obtained
at www.ICGtesting.com
LVHW090549170524
780507LV00038B/558